The Magic Key

Unlock Your Memoir

An Intuitive Guide for New Writers

Anna-Marie O'Brien

The Magic Key

Unlock Your Memoir

Tempe, Arizona
2021

Table of Contents

Woo-Woo Writing Love

Maybe you're a sensitive person, a bit anxious, feeling blocked about your writing, or just plain stuck with where you're at. Maybe you've been struggling with your story for years and are sick of looking for validation from others. Maybe you want to write in a more truthful, heart-centered way, free of the fear of judgement. Maybe you're curious about the concept of "intuitive writing', and how to better engage your own intuition to connect with your story.

Whatever your reasons for being here, welcome.

I wrote this book for people like me - other intuitive, sensitive types who are struggling to write their first book, especially if it's a memoir or a personal narrative.

I searched for years for the secret trick, or the Magic Key, that would unlock the book that felt stuck inside of me. There is a lot of traditional, logical writing advice out there that didn't work, and in fact, made things worse. I know I'm not alone, because I've found that most struggling writers are actually just struggling with bad writing advice.

It was only after I threw that logical advice out the window and started listening to my intuition that I made deep, meaningful progress with my first book. Maybe some of what I share about my experiences will resonate, energetically speaking, and assist you with your first book.

I do talk a lot about energy, vibes, and magic, so if that doesn't feel good or hold some curiosity for you, you probably won't take much away from what I say here. And that's ok - there are multitudes of other writing books that take a different approach and may be a better fit for you.

I'm a librarian, so I know that every book finds its reader, and every writer finds their own process for writing books. As a librarian, I've engaged with writers in my community for close to two decades, and I love nurturing the creative process both in myself and in others. It doesn't matter where you find your inspiration. Resources are everywhere.

But many new writers need a little more support than a book or a free library program can provide, so I've been helping writers as my side-business for three years. I don't really like to call it coaching (I'm not a "sporty" type, so the term feels a little off for me) so I think of it more like morale support for writers. I mostly talk on the phone with new writers who are struggling, who need an empathetic ear, or just a safe place to explore ideas. I also do beta-reading for early drafts, and I'll sometimes offer editing advice on a piece.

As a morale supporter, I want new writers to find joy in the process, and to connect with their own intuition about their writing. I want you to get over the hump and into a productive writing life. Sometimes it does only take one conversation with a person, or one idea from a book, to push past whatever resistance you're experiencing. Learning to trust yourself is a big part of the process.

You probably don't need this book if you are an experienced writer, or have already published a few books, or you are confident about your writing. You probably won't like this book if you are not open to the ideas of magic, serendipity, and energy work.

But, if you ARE struggling AND curious, read on.

Mostly, this book is a collection of ideas and experiences I've shared over the years, with various people who've asked. This is not a "program" of any sort. Mostly it's insights and random things I picked up on my own writing journey. It's the stuff that helped me think of writing in a new way or moved me past an obstacle.

And, although this book mostly refers to writing memoir - I think the ideas here will apply to many types of writing - fiction, narrative nonfiction, and memoir. Take what you need and use it how you see fit. There is no "right way" to write a book.

You just have to find YOUR way.

I offer this up as a bit of a snack to sustain you, made from generous heaps of writing love, with a dash of the woo-woo magic sprinkled on top. Maybe it will provide a little nourishment and encouragement as you pause to read this on your own writing journey.

Chapter Two

Stuck

Obviously, as a librarian, I love books and authors. I'd thought about writing for years, but I didn't know how to be a writer, or how to write a book - it wasn't something that was ever encouraged in my working-class family.

Instead, I just read. Books have always been my constant companion. I've made a career around books. But for so many years, the thought of writing one just seemed so unattainable - and yet, it was always there, calling to me to try.

I successfully avoided my writing urges for years - by moving away to a big city, getting married young, completing a couple of college degrees, settling into a career as a librarian, and having two babies in my late thirties.

But finally, it caught up with me, and I knew my first book had to be a memoir - *Adventures of a Metalhead Librarian* - a story that I'd lived and carried with me for 20 years before I ever felt brave enough to tell it.

So, as I began writing my rock n' roll memoir, I thought it would be an easy, linear process, something logical that I could figure out, just like I did with so many of the college papers I was used to writing. I'd like to think - while quirky in a multitude of ways - that I was a reasonably smart person.

But, when I actually started trying to write the book, I was shocked at how much I felt like a dummy, struggling to get words on the page. Nothing felt right, the writing was stiff and unnatural, and I was crippled by my own self-doubts. I didn't even sound like me.

At the time, all the advice I found was focused on daily habits, word counts, outlines, deadlines, character sketches, stupid writing exercises, "ass in chair" mantras and other tips and tricks to psych yourself into doing the work — and while it all made logical sense, none of it seemed to apply to me in a way that felt "right" in my heart.

I couldn't get comfortable, never felt settled in, didn't have a process, or a framework for even how to approach it. The story I carried around was like a giant, jumbled jigsaw puzzle, dumped out on the floor in the middle of my brain. I had to step around the mess for years, and it was slowly driving me crazy.

Trying to get a first draft done seemed impossible.

Chapter Three

The Vortex of Despair

As I struggled with my story, I reconnected with my old friend, Sam. I'd known him since I was 16, and back in the day, he'd been a long-haired lead singer for a local rock band. Since then, Sam had transformed himself into a successful businessman, sales guru, and motivational speaker. I'd always appreciated his work ethic, and his straightforward style and confidence.

He was a prolific writer, completing three books in two years. He had a nice book deal and a big social media following, did weekly blogs and videos, traveled the country, and made lots of money. A pro in every sense. What was his advice for getting through my book?

"Write every day. Publish every week. Get up at five o'clock in the morning. Calendar out your hours and days so you can schedule time to write. Work out hard. Don't eat carbs." He said this with a bemused smile, half joking, but also dead serious.

Sam, he makes it sound so easy. So logical. While he appears very Zen to people, underneath he's all alpha and is laser-focused on results.

Me, not so much.

Of course, I failed with Sam's advice. I was not laser-focused. Carbs always found me. His kids were grown up, mine in early elementary school. Good grief, I already got up at five a.m. because I had the day job.

I was pushing the boundaries of fatigue and had been for years. I had no idea what to write or publish on a blog - I was just desperate to write my book. I am not alpha. I tend to go with the flow and my mind wanders from task to task. I tend to feel my way through things.

Although I had conformed to being "normal" and jumped through all the performance hoops in order to get through college and a career, I've always known it was a kind of facade, and it wasn't who I really was. It was a persona I played in order to survive in the real world. I've always had "imposter" syndrome, even in my real life.

The real me just wanted to live in a secluded cabin and write books while surrounded by nature and raising chickens.

I mean, I always got things done, but I wasn't hyper about it. I didn't calendar out my days, weeks, months. I tend to think seasonally - in rhythm with the kids' schedules, holidays, vacations. I wrote down important dates as needed. I wrote down what needed to get done, sometimes. And then day by day, I'd do what I needed to do. Not leaps and bounds, but slow steady progress. Nature moves in spirals and waves, and so does my brain.

Sam is extroverted and goal oriented. A-B-C. A guy who likes to compete and win. He commands the spotlight and stage. He's made a boatload of money by developing his confidence, and he hustles his butt off.

But me, I was all seized up with some kind of stage fright. I don't see myself hustling - I just want to connect on a personal level with people. My only goal was to write a book - and maybe a few more in the future if I could just get through the first one.

When I started, I had the opposite of confidence but thought I could "power through" and "lean in" and somehow make it work. So for a while, I still kept the old linear mental expectations, thinking Sam's way had to be the right way because he had great results. *He was a published author with a book deal!*

But trying to implement Sam's advice just led me to guilt, frustration, and feelings of despair as I chased my own tail trying to make it work.

Why? Because I couldn't do it. I couldn't write every day during this stage of my life. I was tired. I had two small kids. I had a job. Because fatigue triggers anxiety and anxiety triggers

perfectionism. And perfectionism triggers despair, and despair triggers paralysis.

It's a nasty vortex to get sucked into. I just wouldn't - couldn't - show myself any mercy. I could sense the pattern, but I couldn't break it.

I know I'm not alone going down this path. I was stuck there for YEARS.

Maybe you're there, now.

And friend, let me tell you, facing a book project without mercy for yourself and in this nasty vortex of despair - is not good. In fact, it's the exact opposite of what was required of me.

I had to figure out how to shift from a shame and despair mindset to an abundance and hope mindset. I didn't know this when I started, of course. It was a process.

And I *knew* it was a process, and the only thing I *knew* I *could* do was to keep pecking away at my story.

Of course, at some point during the writing, it dawned on me that I was trying to apply the wrong advice, from someone I adored, but who was the opposite of me, personality-wise. It doesn't mean it wouldn't work for me at some point, but not then, not under those circumstances, not when I was just starting out and feeling so bound up.

Even so, Sam and I grew up with similar family dynamics and in the same hometown, and the one BIG thing that Sam and I had in common was a work ethic and to NOT QUIT.

I might not be super-confident about a lot of things - but I am STUBBORN when I want something. I know that much.

And I wanted to write the book. I wanted to write the book more than I didn't want to write the book. It was a story that couldn't stay unwritten.

And so, I found a way to exit the vortex of despair, and I wrote the book.

Chapter Four

Find A Way

During this time, as I struggled to get started on my memoir, I read the story of Diana Nyad - the 64-year-old long-distance swimmer who'd completed the grueling 100-mile open-water swim from Cuba to Florida. When asked what got her through the challenge, she shared her mantra: FIND A WAY.

Through exhaustion, jellyfish, sharks, and sunburn:
FIND A WAY.

Through motherhood, a day-job, and health issues:
 FIND A WAY.

I wrote that mantra on a sticky note and posted it on my computer monitor. FIND A WAY.

That little sticky on my monitor worked. I started feeling like maybe it was actually possible to write the book. And as I kept pecking, finding my way, I remembered a few things about who I really was.

I remembered that I had a deep and meaningful connection to my intuition and unconscious mind. That I could often "read" energy and manifest positive outcomes.

I remembered that my dreams often connected me to people through time and space.

I remembered that I'd had intense and magical energetic experiences that had guided me my whole life, and especially in the story about which I wanted to write.

I remembered that I believed in magic.

I remembered my ancestors who didn't give up.

I remembered that I'm a librarian who is surrounded by tens of thousands of books that started off as dreams, written by writers who found a way to write them. I saw it every day, the evidence of all possibilities - if you just don't quit.

I remembered that anything I had ever really wanted to do - I found a way to do.

Writing the book was no different.

Sam found a way to write his books. His ideas and methods worked for him.

And eventually, I found a way to write my book. I found ideas and methods that worked for me. Once size does not fit all when it comes to writing. You keep trying things and eventually, you dig in and make progress. So fast or slow, organized or sloppy, confident or not so much - it's time to find YOUR way.

Chapter Five

Intuition and the Push & Pull

So, look. We all have intuitive gifts.

Intuition is part of who we are, as humans. It's built into our DNA and is a natural, needed part of us - our 6th sense. Intuition is a tool of survival. Our gut feelings often keep us safe, and alive.

Our intuition gives us valuable information. We all know this.

However, in our data-driven, results-oriented, busy-busy world, intuition is not a skill that gets credit for results. Intuition isn't even really acknowledged as a skill set at all.

For a regular day-job, no one puts *"I'm intuitive, so I just know things"* on their resume or application. We often subvert our natural intuition with overbearing logic out of necessity and economic obligations. Intuition is a soft skill that human resource departments can't even describe.

Personally, I think intuition is THE skill to develop and trust if you're starting out as a writer.

What I found when I went looking for traditional writing advice is that it is dominated by logic, word count, strict writing routines, and it's always focused on constant, relentless productivity. Hard skill. Hard effort. Hard pushing. Goals goals goals. Deadlines. WORK.

This is a very masculine energy mindset. This is my friend Sam's way.

Masculine energy is needed in the world, obviously. We have to actually <u>do</u> the work, and writing <u>is</u> work, and there is absolutely nothing wrong with logic, habit, or progress. We need it to write books, and we need it for balance and survival.

We have to be able to think rationally about the world around us and taking a logical approach to writing is natural for many different kinds of writers. They get things written, and if they have found their sweet spot, I'm happy for them. They have found a way to do their work.

But here's the thing - there is a push and a pull to writing, and hard logic and pushing yourself doesn't work for every writer.

<u>Especially</u> new writers and/or highly sensitive types just starting their memoirs or personal narratives about possibly sensitive and painful topics. Memoirs have a way of dredging up ancestral trauma, abuse, addiction, betrayal, and many of the

other transformations, realizations, and hard lessons learned while going through an interesting life and wanting to write about some of it.

Pushing yourself too fast and too soon can actually shut you down and lock up the magic of the story you need to share. Pushing can be crippling to us sensitive, empathic, anxious, or intuitive types.

So, you may think you are in a PUSH phase when you start your memoir, but you are not, and you shouldn't be.

You are actually trying to PULL the story to you, collecting clues, attracting the information, people, and insights that you need to write the book. It's a gathering of forces, so to speak.

This is not the time for pushing. The act of writing out your story is a type of deep therapy, and healing can come in waves as you knit it all together and sort it all out. If you push too soon, some of the insights and connections get lost because you haven't relaxed and allowed the information to be revealed to you in a way that will really connect you to the heart of your story.

Even humorous or lighthearted memoirs have painful and awkward moments that need to be examined. Misunderstandings, ironies, heartbreaks, reckonings. No life is spotless, and trust me, a lot of stuff will bubble up on you as you begin to write it out.

It can take time to process the emotions and information you're gathering, both as a human being and as a writer. And if you're stuck or not sure how to move forward, it's best not to set

Beautiful

16

a deadline, or any expectations or goals on this work right now. You are going deep, rather than broad, and it can take time to mine the depths of your heart and psyche.

So, don't push yet.

The pushing phase comes later, after you've completed a few drafts, and during the editing and production.

Chapter Six

Have Mercy

If you're all bound up and feeling bad about your writing, it's time to approach the work with a different mindset. Let's relax a bit and cut ourselves a break.

Have mercy for yourself, friend.

It's time to unclench and let go of all the baggage around your writing. Maybe we approach it with a more feminine, receptive energy. Nurturing. With love, forgiveness, understanding.

The book you want to write is really your love child. Treat it gently.

Treat *yourself* gently.

You are in the process of birthing that love child. This is all feeling and discovery and faith. The love child is setting the agenda and the timeline. You are here to facilitate, protect, and nurture. You are here to submit to the divine process of creation.

love child

18

And of course, there are times when you need to push, to bear down and lean into it and move the load forward. But not now, not yet. There is a time and place for pushing, and you'll know when.

If you're just starting out trying to write a book, the goal is to develop a relationship between intuition (pulling) and logic (pushing) so that you can cultivate the writing life and ethos that works for you and produces the outcomes you want.

But while you're trying to get that first hard, ugly, crazy draft down on paper, let it all go. Let go of your own expectations. Just surrender yourself to discovery. Trust the process. Let your own inner wisdom and intuition guide you forward.

surrender

The love child - your book - has an energy force of its own, and it's connected to you at the heart. It can't speak full words right now - but you can understand what it's telling you if you keep your channels open and listen. It wants to be born in its truest form. And that can only come from you, the creator.

As a benevolent creator, you must have mercy on yourself and your story.

Don't push it around and demand results of it. Pull it close and nurture it. Speak to it with love, and it will answer in a most profound way.

Writing your first draft of a memoir is HEART work. Not BRAIN work.

Chapter Seven

My Magic Key

I did, at some point, seriously wonder what was wrong with me, writing wise. I felt so stuck with my memoir. But the thought of asking for help caused me a lot of anxiety. I've been that way my whole life - I hate admitting that I need help. Maybe it's because I was raised by people - Sicilian immigrants - who thought asking for help was a sign of weakness. You didn't talk about your problems to strangers, you kept things in the family. I'd never done any kind of therapy or counseling. You tough it out, and you figure it out. This isn't always the healthiest mindset, of course, but it's what I knew and how I survived.

Struggling and feeling bad about my writing felt totally normal.

I also knew that writing groups were definitely not my thing. Not only was I a busy working mom who couldn't take the time to go meet people at a coffee shop, I felt very protective of my story. It was sex, drugs, rock n' roll. A few famous people were involved. The thought of sharing this story with a group of strangers felt very, very wrong to me.

So, while searching around for answers, killing time and not writing, I took a personality test - The Meyers-Briggs. Although I'd done various tests over the years, this one, at this time, really resonated with me.

I came up INFJ, and as I researched more about it, I felt like I finally had some answers about why I was having a hard time writing my book.

One day, I typed in "INFJ writing" into the search bar and I found Lauren. She was a writer, and she was offering her services as a writing coach. She worked exclusively with intuitive types and introverts - mostly other INFJ's just like me.

I was intrigued of course, but I had never thought of coaching. I wasn't a team sports kind of person, and really disliked feeling like I needed "coaching" (again with the Sicilian pride thing) but, I had a hunch. I took a chance and I contacted her.

Thank goodness I did because we clicked instantly. There was nothing "coach-y" about Lauren at all. Just gentle support and love and helpful insights. Unconditional and focused. She totally got my woo-woo ways. She did not think I was crazy when I told her about my premonitions and dreams, or about my Tarot cards, or that I tracked the phases of the moon. I finally found someone who understood me - as a person and as a writer.

Gosh, to feel understood, sometimes, is everything.

And I learned SO much.

You know that old saying - "when the student is ready, the teacher will appear"...? Well, Lauren showed up right when I needed her.

As you keep going, you'll find that this happens often - what you need shows up right on time to help you with the next step.

So, I started to find my writing voice, literally, by talking on the phone to someone who had been through the same experience - who had been stuck on bad advice, who had written a revealing memoir and was *also* writing transgressive fiction - courageous ventures, both - and who worked with writers who struggled with the very same things as I did.

Lauren was really on to something with her approach. She knew that working with and trusting your intuition is the best way to unlock your story when nothing else seems to work.

I felt like I had been given permission to just be who I was as a writer.

This was Lauren's way. Feminine, receptive, nurturing.

This is the way that really opened the doors for me. This was my Magic Key, learning to trust my intuition and my own internal compass.

Talking to another writer helped me learn the language of writing and to discover what I was actually trying to say.

Lauren was my first beta reader during those early, ugly drafts, and she saw themes and patterns I had not considered.

She helped me shift from the vortex of despair into a hope and abundance mindset.

She held space for me over many years as I slogged away at my book, and guess what? I got my writing done.

We only talked on the phone every three or four months, and emailed in spurts to keep in touch, and it was really all I needed. A gentle, trusted, non-judgmental, supportive person. A writing friend who wanted me to succeed.

Finding this one person to talk to about writing, about all the things I was encountering - both the emotional, the mechanical, the hopes and fears - my writing coach, Lauren, was my secret weapon against the vortex of despair.

She was worth ten times more than the reasonable amount I paid her for her time.

She is also the reason I eventually started working with other writers as a writing coach myself, although I'm still sketchy on the "coach" term. I like "morale supporter" much better, but it's not as succinct as "coach".

Whatever we call it, I'm helping people unlock their own intuition about their books, just like Lauren helped me unlock mine. I couldn't do this work if I hadn't been through the process.

Like me, the writers I've worked with over the years don't want another self-help program or empty promises of great success. Mostly they just want someone to talk to about writing and all the complexities of writing a book, and that's what I offer to writers who find me.

Maybe it's a good friend, or a spouse, or a therapist, or a mentor for you, but for me, I was happy to find another writer who understood exactly what I was struggling with. Who didn't put me on a program or make me sign a contract or cluck at me when I was stuck or suggest I do meaningless writing exercises when I really just wanted to work on my book.

None of that. Just enjoyable, supportive, funny conversations with a person who got me.

However you do it, I would encourage you to find your writing person. More than any credentials or credits, the most important qualification for a writing coach is that they are a writer or creative, that you like them as a human, and that they feel good to you, like an old friend and someone you can trust.

Finding a writing coach (or a morale supporter) was a huge Magic Key. It's what really helped me unlock my writing, and I'll bet it could help you, too.

Chapter Eight

The Intuitive Memoir

In talking with countless readers and writers over the years, many people think a memoir is a "biography", or an "autobiography" and it is not.

Not always, but those are usually reserved for famous people, and the book would cover the span of their entire life.

A memoir is a bit different.

A memoir isn't the story *of* your entire life, it's the story of a time *in* your life.

A moment of clarity, change, a metamorphosis, a snapshot of a moment and a place and a thing that you did, that happened to you, or that you learned from.

Of course, there will be backstory, and connections to other parts of your life, but the basis of the memoir itself is an event, a time, a change, a challenge, a discovery.

Whether it's a light, fun story, or a deep, dark dive – your memoir is a story of what you were before, during, and after that moment, that place, or that thing you did or that happened to you. In other words, there's a timeframe, and a transformation to explain.

An autobiography goes wide across a life. A memoir goes deep into one pivotal experience.

This narrows your focus quite a bit. You don't have to write about every dang thing over the span of your life and try to make it all make sense. You might refer to certain events from the past and tie them in, but only if it serves the story, or the thing, the transformation, the discovery, that you're writing the memoir about.

Going a bit slower and using your intuition in this process can bring out textures, themes, colors, and moods that will help connect your story to readers in a deeper, more soul-gratifying way.

So basically, what I'm calling an "Intuitive Memoir" is one that you write in a receptive, open state. You follow the rhythm of the story and allow it to guide you through to its full gestation.

It's not a reporting of facts so much as it is a discovery of meaning.

You ask for guidance, and it appears naturally, and in a way you recognize. You listen to your body and what it's telling you. You recognize signs, you notice coincidences, and dreams, and

memoir / biography

Intuitive ·

✳ discovery of meaning

Beautiful

the people they're connected to. You connect with the right people at the right time.

It's writing in a state of intention, awareness, acceptance, gratitude and wonder. It is writing that is truthful - but not vindictive.

And then you put that writing into a sequence that readers will understand and enjoy, because like any other book, **memoir is meant to be a story in service to the reader.** *Service*

This is important work, whether you realize it or not. Your true story can impact lives and inform generations. Your authenticity and vulnerability are required.

Good memoir speaks truth in a way that enlightens and connects. A good memoir is written with love for the story, for the humanity involved, for the impact and connection it will have with the reader.

You can't really do this in a vortex of despair, or with a hard deadline, or pushing yourself with daily writing goals. You do it by trusting what comes through as you write. Sometimes it's just better to "write slow" and give it some air. You'll start writing faster as you work your way through drafts.

For as good as it feels to actually write the memoir - however long it takes - it is a *much* greater reward to know that it connected emotionally with people and served a purpose greater than your own self-satisfaction for having done it.

Writing and publishing your first book is a life-changing experience. Transformative, maybe even more so than the event you're writing about.

It takes a lot of courage to go digging up old bones, and to expose yourself in the town square, so to speak. But, when you do the work and ask for guidance, when you open up and really connect with your story, you serve a purpose much greater than yourself.

And when you work with purpose and love and in service to others, the Universe responds in ways that can feel like Big Magic.

Chapter Nine

Big Magic Vibes

While I was writing my memoir, I really, really needed to talk to Kevin, one of my closest friends from back in the day who had been there with me and was witness to much of my story.

Problem was, I couldn't find him. I hadn't talked to him since 1994. He had no digital footprint and wasn't on the socials. Maybe he'd shaved his head and moved to Argentina, for all I knew. I looked everywhere, connecting with old mutual friends to try to and get a message to him. It was like chasing a phantom.

So, as I kept going, I made a list of all the things I needed to talk to Kevin about. Two years into writing and about half-way through my second draft, I went to bed one night, kind of stumped, wondering how I could really continue writing the book without his input. I was so sad about it.

I needed to ask him so many questions - about people, places, events, his memories and impressions. Plus, I just wanted to talk to my old friend. Writing the story was bringing up stuff that I knew only Kevin would understand.

Anyways, that night, after feeling disheartened about not connecting with Kevin for all those years, I went on to have a very specific and intense dream about him.

I found him in a big leafy park, walking alone in his black leather jacket. He still had his long brown hair. I was so happy to see my old friend, handsome and healthy.

In the dream I told him: "Kevin, I really, really need to talk to you about my book. I need your help". We sat down on a park bench in the crisp fall air with orange leaves all around, and we started catching up. It was a lovely, comforting dream. He'd always felt like a brother to me.

I woke up the next morning feeling so much better. Isn't it funny how dreams can do that? I poured my coffee and logged in to my computer.

I was stunned to see that there was a Facebook friend request and a message from Kevin.

He called me that day, we talked for over two hours, I asked him all my questions, he beta-read my almost-done drafts, he sent me funny memes to keep my spirits up while I finished the book, and we picked up our friendship like no time had passed at all.

Holy cow, Big Magic!

We need to talk about magic, and what I mean when I use the word.

After working with writers for years as a librarian and having gone through the book-writing process myself, I now have this idea in my head that the books we want to write already exist, fully formed, within us.

I believe they have a consciousness and a soul of their own, and they want to be born into a physical form, through us. When I talk about magic, and intuition, I think this is how we connect and listen to that consciousness, that specific creative energy inside us that is waiting to be born into a book.

Humans are energetic beings. Various religious and esoteric practices over the years reflect the dynamics of this energy – prayer, meditation, or focused practice on a skill – all are efforts to connect with "The Force" in some way. Some call it God or Allah or Yeshua. Some think of it in female terms – Mother Earth, or the Goddess, or Gaia.

In reality, it encompasses both male and female creative energy.

And look, everything is energy. Everything vibrates. We are all connected by it. We are all a part of a "collective unconscious" Our human energy is tied to every other energetic life force, whether we know it or not. Planets have energy, the sun has energy, water has energy, earth has energy. People, animals, trees, books, places. All carry and emit energy. The experiences and wisdom of our ancestors carry energy.

Our thoughts have an energetic signature that exists independent of time and space.

Maybe it will help to think of yourself, your entire body, as a giant receiver, amplifier, and transmitter. We can learn to tune in to the different energy channels. We can learn to recognize the messages that come through both through our regular senses, and our extra-senses.

Our job as a writer is to pay attention and notice what is coming through.

Energetic vibes coming through to you don't necessarily connect to this dimension as we know it. It isn't logical or linear. It's just there, waiting for you to tune in to it, to recognize it, to resonate. People have different ways of reading the energy - some feel it, some hear it, some see it, some dream it.

And once you start to recognize these things - doors open in your mind, and momentum builds. You are directing your thoughts - your energy - towards receiving important information from new sources.

It can take time to feel comfortable doing this, recognizing patterns, and understanding the connections. Sometimes it's very obvious, sometimes it's a creeper. Each of us must decide what information is useful for the story.

The more you pay attention, the more magic shows up. The more you trust this magic, the more guidance you receive. In other words – the more you expect it, the more you experience it. The more you write it down, the more you make it happen.

32

The more you pray for it – well, you get the idea. I found that when I asked directly for specific help – it would materialize in a variety of ways.

So, basically, magic is a general term for the unexplained benevolence and good will that shows up when you ask for help and actively engage in the sacred ritual of writing your story.

And the Big Magic didn't just happen with my friend Kevin, when I dreamed of him and then woke up to a Facebook message from him in the morning after more than 25 years of distance. I have dozens of examples of this force at work, both in my real life and my writing life.

And when it shows up, it feels magical, miraculous, perfect.

The Universe will conspire to help you if you ask and if you take action. Just remember to be specific about what it is you really want.

Write it all down and see what happens.

Chapter Ten

Analog & Digital

I am Generation X, the last generation to have a truly analog childhood. I remember what "back in the day" was like. It was an analog world, with a digital future. We had to learn decent penmanship and we didn't learn to type until high school, where we learned on old IBM Selectrics.

I didn't own a computer until I was 22, and I didn't get a cell phone until I was 30. The technological advances we've adapted to have changed so much of our daily routine. It enriches our lives in many ways, and as an information junkie, I love being connected like this.

But, but, but...there is a price. We are so entrenched in our screens and digital life. Digital distractions are very, very real. Especially to us anxious, ADD/OCD sensitive types. I am very aware of the periods of mindless doom-scrolling on my phone.

It's changed our brains, our health, and our creativity. And as writers and creatives we have to be honest about how our digital use affects us. How many more hours a day do you need to spend in front of a screen?

We all know the blue light of screens is bad for your brain. It interferes with your circadian rhythms and melatonin production, both of which are crucial to good sleep.

Good sleep is where the good dreams and deep insights are. If you're writing a memoir, this dreamtime is a goldmine of intuitive information. Try to protect it and nurture it.

So, while there is no doubt you'll be keyboarding and doing a lot of screen time while writing a book, I do want to advocate for breaks from it. It's nice to step away and use our hands to do "real" stuff.

Like making dinner, or art.

We often overlook our hands. They are beautiful, analog, sensory instruments, capable of transmitting so much information to the brain. Keyboard clicks aren't the same as doing work by hand, washing dishes by hand, building things by hand, cooking by hand, painting by hand, weeding the garden by hand, or writing by hand.

Doing handwork and chores can put our brains into a semi-meditative state, where our thoughts wander in the dishwater, where we can connect insights as we push a vacuum, and where we come up with a timeline as we hang up a load of laundry or

35

water the plants. Some of the most creative minds in the world have been hit with amazing ideas just by doing some chores.

Our brains are analog, animal, kinetic, and intuitive. Analog activity engages our monkey brain with the task at hand while our unconscious mind figures out the deep problems and finds the missing connections.

This is why it's good to unplug and go analog. The idea is to put your subconscious mind to work on a problem while you get other things done.

This is part of writing a book. Even if you aren't sitting there physically typing out your book, your brain is still writing the book and figuring things out. Even if you know you're procrastinating a bit – at least make it a productive procrastination. Enjoy the analog time and then get back to work when you're ready.

This is progress, even if it takes a while for the word count to catch up.

Chapter Eleven

The Good Enough Principle

I know writers who never write by hand - it all goes into some kind of digital productivity system - and I also know writers who do all of their drafting by longhand, in spiral notebooks or on legal pads.

You probably fall somewhere in the middle on using the keyboard for everything or writing things down analog style. Maybe you already have some kind of a hybrid mindset, like I do. Whatever works, works.

My training as a librarian wants systems and indexes and tags and metadata. So, if left to ponder for too long - I really overthink these things and get a little obsessive. I struggled for a good long while trying to find the best balance of:

1. Perfectly organized searchable digital files in Evernote and on my desktop, and

2. A flawless, pristine bullet-journal type notebook into which all of my creative notes would be beautifully arranged, indexed, curated and decorated with fancy markers.

Of course I realized that I was not capable of either ideal. Fussing over the organization of everything was really just a huge distraction from doing the *actual* writing work.

Perfectionism will kill your creative spirit.

So, now I just focus on the writing work, and figure out the organization - if any - later on. My desktop gets messy, then I batch things into files when it starts to bug me.

I've never not been able to find something I needed.

I know it probably sounds weird for a librarian who loves organizational systems, but it's true. I fuss over that stuff in my professional life.

For my writing life, I don't want to. I don't care. It doesn't matter. What matters is the actual writing and getting the book done. Who cares how organized my files or notebooks were while I was learning how to write a book?

Mostly it would be just me who cared, and I don't.

Well, I *decided* not to care. Sometimes you must draw a line in the sand and let things go.

You kind of have to untrain yourself.

What I've learned from myself, and from sensitive writers like me is:

Perfectionism is not productive. In fact, it's just the opposite. It can impede progress, especially during the first draft.

This also relates to the "planning vs. pantsing" debate that so many writers engage in. Which is - is it better to free write, or to write according to a plan that you've already figured out?

Of course this will be different for every writer, and maybe even for every book. At first, I LOVED the idea of having a plan to follow. It made logical sense. But for my first book, it was totally not necessary.

I do like to write things down, journal, have a loose map, or a list of ideas I want to cover. It helps me feel less anxious, less dependent upon my brain to remember.

At one point, I had a stack of index cards with different scenes I wanted to include. At another point, I had a bunch of stuff on colored sticky notes, stuck to a wall so I could visualize, like a puzzle.

Doing those things helped me figure out a problem. It wasn't a plan.

What I realized was that for me to spend the time making a big organized book plan with an outline and then trying to live up to it and keeping things in the right order and staying on track with a deadline - the pressure is too much. It's pushing too much on parts that sometimes need to be coaxed out of hiding.

Maybe for future books, having a book plan will work. But right now, while you're struggling to get a first draft of a first book done – just relax.

For me, it's mostly that I do not want to trigger my anxiety or perfectionism. I do not want to set myself up for failure. I don't want to obsess over making a plan and sticking to it.

I want to obsess over the actual writing, and I want it to flow, unimpeded by the pressure of perfect organization or logic. I want flexibility, not rigidity. I want freedom to explore. I want to play, to be joyful, to discover.

So, for me, it had to be an intentional and willful "letting go" of plans and perfectionism - and making 'good enough' my new rule. Good enough lets you move on to the next thing you need to work on.

I'd rather have a good enough finished book than a perfect unfinished idea for a book. Got it?

You are a good enough writer. You will write a good enough draft. You will keep good enough notes and files. You will write and finish a good enough book, and you'll be thrilled that you did it.

You won't be the same person you were when you started.

You'll be free of the fear of failure. Because now you know you can do it.

Acceptance of the Good Enough Principle is *enormously* liberating. **'Good enough' keeps the intuitive channels open. Perfectionism shuts them down.**

Chapter Twelve

The Imperfect Notebook

All that said, I do think every writer probably needs some kind of writing notebook, grimoire, or commonplace journal.

Information never comes to me in an exact order, so this is a place to capture random bits for the book. A place to jot down ideas, journal entries, lists, dates, passwords - whatever needs written down.

I jot notes about the day. Dreams. My daily Tarot card pull. Things I want to follow up on. Notes from podcasts, or books I'm reading. Weird interactions or people. Observations. Just, whatever. I use sticky notes and highlighters as needed, but then I move on.

It's a workhorse, a catch-all, and a trusted companion. When I'm done with one notebook, I save it in a storage bin along with other scraps, printouts, random notes and sticky's that I want to save from that time. I keep the bin near my writing desk, so I can dig for it if needed. This is fertile soil. I think of it as a kind of "idea farm".

I try not to get too precious or fancy with my notebooks because during their lifespan, they get tossed into a big purse with a bunch of other stuff as I go about my day as a mom and librarian. I'm capturing tidbits, observing life, leaving myself some breadcrumbs for the future.

I sometimes refer to myself as OCD + ADD + ESP - and a writing notebook helps me manage it. I like simplicity, so keeping my random bits together in one place helps the OCD, being able to jot things down while distracted helps the ADD, and having a place to record the clues that show up is great for the ESP.

Composition books work well for this. So do spiral bound. My only requirement is that my notebook should have a good sturdy cover, and graph paper. I often like to doodle, and I find the graph paper works well with my non-linear brain.

I also adore a good Flair or felt-tip pen. Black ink only.

That's it. That's as much as I fuss about my notebook. It's imperfect. It's messy. It's helpful, and it's good enough. Someday my kids can go through the bins of notebooks and marvel at all the random crap that their mom saved.

Over the years, I've known writers who keep separate notebooks for every dang thing. They have like, six beautiful, organized notebooks going at all times. Character notebooks, scene notebooks, weather notebooks, quote notebooks, journals, dream diaries - all that.

And if it works for them, then great. I'm in awe of that kind of dedication to notebooks.

I don't keep a set of notebooks or get too fancy, because:

1. I'd spend more time curating my notebooks than I would actually working on the book, and once my 'perfectionism' trigger is clicked, I'll get obsessive, and I'll freeze, and then I'll flail about for a while. I really can't tell you how many beautiful blank notebooks I ruined before I figured this out - but it's been A LOT. Once I mess one up, I have to start over, and I hate that feeling.

2. Keeping perfect notebooks perpetuates the illusion of control over the creative process, fetishizes busy-ness, and almost - narciss-izes the ideas - which is the exact opposite of what we are trying to conjure up by using our intuition.

A really brilliant insight comes through and then I'm going to fuss over where to write it down, with which pen, in my best handwriting, in the correct notebook? Gah. These days I just jot it down in the everyday imperfect notebook, or on a sticky that I then put in the notebook.

We really need to shake loose from our perfectionist control tendencies, stop being so busy-busy, and just record things as they come, refer to them as needed, and move on to a new notebook when necessary. Save the notebooks and go back through from time to time. You'll find some real gems for your writing life.

But don't be obsessive about it. Just be cool.

There is no gold star for pretty notebooks.

The point in even keeping a writer's notebook is to establish an open and helpful relationship with your intuitive brain. The point is to train your brain to relax and receive using your notebook and pen as a tool for creativity. To observe the curiosities. To collect the information. To connect the patterns. To leave yourself some clues. To trust what shows up - and believe me, a lot will show up if you just relax.

Keep your imperfect notebooks as messy, or as neat as you like. As long as it makes you happy and is useful. It's a tool to enhance the book-writing process, which is your focus.

Keeping a perfect notebook is NOT the focus.

Set your mind to the book you want to write, not the notebook you want to keep.

The bottom line is - It's not so much *how* you write things down, or where, or how neatly - it's the ACTUAL ACT of writing things down - BY HAND - that is important.

44

Chapter Thirteen

Write It Down Make It Happen

Maybe it was the old classic *Think and Grow Rich* by Napoleon Hill - but it was a long time ago in a book that I first came across the concept of writing your dreams and goals down by hand. I was struck by the simplicity of the concept, and how it was described as "almost magic".

Then, I found a book called *Write It Down, Make It Happen* by Henriette Anne Klauser. And the more I was intrigued by the concept, the more books about it showed up.

I know it doesn't sound all that remarkable, writing things down by hand - but it is. Every time I engaged in this practice with intention, really awesome things would manifest.

I guess they call it "The Law of Attraction" these days. To me, it's a type of prayer. It's using "The Force".

Basically, it's the concept that what you put out into the world is what you attract back to yourself.

As human beings in a multi-dimensional Universe, we are, indeed, giant energetic receivers and transmitters.

And because of this, it's important to be aware of what you are putting out into the world, and what you let in. What you actively allow into your energy field can and will affect you.

For me, I can't watch or read a lot of violence or horror or anything related to zombies. I have physical reactions to this stuff, and I don't want to set my vibes lower or occupy my limited brain capacity with things that bring me down, scare me, or gross me out. I do not want my mind in a "fight or flight" mode.

Instead, I seek out calmness, beauty, and laughter, and I find examples and inspiration everywhere.

Purposefully minding your energy to radiate towards the positive will likewise attract good things to you. Hang around low-vibing people, and you start to vibe lower.

Energy is contagious - it's a sympathetic resonance.

I'm not saying writing things down is a be-all end-all for your writing life. It's not some kind of parlor trick. You must want it, and work for it. It requires action.

I've had many people over the years tell me *"Oh, I tried doing the Law of Attraction and it just doesn't work for me"*. Well, I'm not going to psychoanalyze that, but my hunch is there are blocks in other ways, energetically. The person is passively waiting for a result to be gifted.

Writing your goals/ideas/dreams down, with a pen on paper is action, and makes them suddenly "real". Your ideas now have a form, a mass, and a weight attached to them from the ink and the paper. Your thoughts are now "things" and have an energetic signature that is heavier than the ether of your brain.

Writing requires intention, and it imprints the energy of that intention upon your brain and aura. When you remind yourself often of that intention, your energy begins to align to it. You start to level up.

Besides, you cannot receive anything you really want if you haven't asked for it in your life. This is how prayers are answered.

Sometimes, it can take YEARS for things to happen. But sometimes it all comes together quickly, and it does seem magical. Sometimes maybe even like a miracle.

So in your imperfect notebook or journal, take the time to write out your visions, goals, dreams, desires. Prime the pump and get things flowing. This is a process that requires ACTION toward the dream or goal. It's literally a part of the word "attrACTION".

And, you wouldn't have the urge to write your book if you weren't truly capable of doing it. Writing things down may be a tiny little action, but it IS action and can start forward motion.

Tell the Universe exactly what you want and ask the Universe to provide you with what you need.

I wrote down a list of things to ask my friend, Kevin, with the intention of being ready for him when he showed up. I didn't know WHEN he'd show up, but somehow I knew he would if I asked him to, in an energetic sense.

He showed up.

Writing things down is like a bat-signal. This is action.

Write down how you want to feel. Action.

Ask for help. Be specific. Action.

Show up and start writing your book, no matter how awful or awkward you feel, even if it's just for an hour a week. Action.

Treat your desire to write this book a sacred thing. Honor it and trust it.

You will be provided with everything you need. The Universe will answer. The Universe *always* answers. Just have faith and pay attention. And keep writing things down by hand.

Writing things down by hand is the place to begin if you don't know where else to begin.

Chapter Fourteen

A Word About Drafts

If you're a new writer, it feels weird to start writing a book - it's clunky, awkward, and you really don't know if you're doing it right.

Believe me, if you're not sure if you're doing it right - you are absolutely doing it right.

There are no hard rules here. The goal is to get through a first draft so that you have something to edit.

I will tell you, though, expect to save some drafts as you begin to write on your computer.

OK, ALOT of drafts.

My first assumption about writing was that it would be a clean, linear, and organized process, but it was not. I feel like it took me days to settle in, to really start working on a piece. I was

doing it right (handwritten margin note)

all over the place. It was circular, spiral, and wavy. I stopped for weeks, and then I'd start again.

I found myself wanting to start my writing sessions by cleaning things up where I left off. A few minutes of tweaking seemed to get my head back into the writing.

But don't worry too much about hardcore editing right now. Tweak a few things to get back into the draft, don't get bogged down too much. Just get some more words down.

Once your book is done, you'll see that you worked on what needed to be worked on, when it was supposed to be worked on. Just remember to save as you go.

Of course, I didn't realize how many drafts of the book I'd be writing and saving, or how many sections I'd rewrite, or remove or move around and resave.

This is part of doing the work. It can get messy. It can feel like chaos, especially if you're still wrangling with perfectionism. BUT THIS IS PART OF THE PROCESS.

Just keep working. Even when you're paused with the writing, your brain is going to be working. Gathering information, processing, researching, incubating, and connecting.

I had what I would consider about ten first drafts. I wrote and fixed, wrote and fixed. I had to do this quite a few times, and it got easier as I kept doing it. The 10th draft of my first draft was much better than the first draft of my first draft.

I almost lost my entire nerve when I realized I needed to tear the whole thing apart scene-by-scene. Gosh, that was HARD. It was like a badly sewn quilt that I had to rip up, trim, and rearrange in a more solid fashion. Some of it didn't make the cut.

But I had to trust the process and do that work.

And then I had a second draft.

And the tenth draft of my second draft was much better than my first draft of my second draft.

More tearing and rending apart. It can feel brutal. Tough love.

"Kill your darlings" is a true phrase. Sometimes you sacrifice bits of your story that you love in order to make it a better story. You'll have a few great scenes that you'll figure out don't actually belong.

More drafts saved.

Sometimes, it can take a while for a book to work its way out of you. It took me two years of struggling plus five full years writing and editing. It was almost like getting another college degree, learning how to write a book.

But, I learned what I needed to learn. Every book you write will teach you something and eventually you'll know when you're done. You'll know it in your bones.

Create as many drafts as you need. Just remember to back up your work as you go.

Chapter Fifteen

Story Structure & Metaphysical Mechanics

After I slogged through my first awkward draft, I couldn't figure out why my book wasn't working. I had tons of chapters that didn't seem connected.

And only then – after I had a solid first draft - did I started researching story structure.

It hadn't occurred to me before then. I just needed to get that first draft out of me.

I had to create the parts first, and then figure out where to put them in the puzzle later – which might seem counter to logic.

Because it is. If you're a planner or an outliner, you design the puzzle first, and then chop it up into parts.

Another way to think of being a planner/outliner is like having an architect draw a design for a house. You figure out where everything is supposed to go before you build. Then, all the parts are gathered and joined together according to the design plan. This is efficient, obviously. The creativity is done on the front end, during the design phase. You order the exact supplies you need, nothing more. Everything from there is just labor. But if something needs changed structurally, the entire design needs shifted.

Instead of hard planning/outlining, freewriting all the parts into a first draft is like being let loose in a wild forest with an ax and a wheelbarrow. You chop and drag and do all the labor up front, gathering logs and stones to build your house.

This is your first draft.

When you have everything laid out in the field, *then* you start designing your house from what you've gathered, using your creativity and intuition to guide you into finding the structure.

Where do the parts *really* belong? Often, they won't tell you until *after* they're written.

You may decide not to use certain parts, but it doesn't mean you didn't need to write them. On some deep level, those parts are trying to communicate with you about the real meaning, lesson, or theme of the story. Write them out in a way that feels good to you and figure out where to put them and how to connect them, later. Or toss them out if it turns out you don't need them. Every part you use needs to have a purpose in the story.

First Draft (chop logs carry water)

intuition & structure

And so, when my first draft was finally written, I went looking for answers about how to arrange it all effectively – how to build the house.

I learned that there are only a few basic story structures. When you stretch out a book and break it down scene by scene into the common patterns of human perception, you can see that stories have shapes.

Kurt Vonnegut wrote his master's thesis on this concept. There are now computer models of the major story structures, applied across all kinds of literature and film.

It changes everything once you realize it. I had no idea that most Hollywood films follow a set formula, and that we are wired as humans for certain patterns in a story.

As a reader, the story structure is often invisible, but as a writer, it's a thing. It's a BIG thing. Putting the story parts in their correct order and arranging it in a familiar sequence is a huge service to the reader.

Honestly, it was mind boggling to me. Like, duh. What the heck. *How did I not know this?* I'm a librarian for goodness' sake!

Writing a memoir is no different than any other book. It can have a structure very similar to fiction. It still has a beginning, a middle, and an end. It has a protagonist (you) and an inciting incident, action and dialog and transitions and tension and resolution.

Even if you are writing your memoir as a series of vignettes or short stories, there will be these elements in each of the stories, as well as an arc tying them all together into a larger theme.

Once I understood how *A* story was supposed to work, then I knew how I could make *MY* story work. I already had the major parts written in the draft - even as placeholders - and now I just had to rearrange them. And then I knew what else I had to write to connect the parts.

Once I started thinking about structure, I wasn't writing or editing blindly. I could think about each part of my story, and where best to start each section, and where to end it. I helped me write with purpose and intent, and in a way that would be easy and pleasurable for the reader.

So, based on my experience my view is that you should have a first draft done before you start flexing on structure. Because you need something to work with. And you're on a path of discovery here, too. You need a little room to stretch when you're writing memoir.

Trust yourself. Trust your story. It will guide you. Sometimes you just need to play with it to find its true shape and form. Play with it a bit to see what needs to be done. Your book will show you the way. The structure will find you.

You might need to do a little more work and a little more tweaking as you build the house, but it allows so much room for magic, revelation, depth and beauty. You adjust as you go, tightening things up.

I know it might sound overly logical, analyzing story parts. Maybe even counter intuitive. But my goodness, once I had my ugly first draft done and I understood that I had to put it all in human order, once I could see how to build the story according to a recognizable pattern, my writing flowed with purpose.

Seeing the shapes of stories helped me SO MUCH. Maybe the idea will help you, too.

It was another Magic Key that unlocked my writing

Chapter Sixteen

Scenes First, Chapters Later

Related to structure, a big problem I had in my early drafts was thinking that I had to write everything into chapters.

I had the chapters outlined and named, and a few notes as to what would happen in each chapter. I thought this is what writers did.

Maybe some do. I just know it wasn't working for me. Once written, my chapters were flabby and not held together well.

Now, as a reader, chapters make sense. They are commonly used and a familiar and comfortable way to organize the parts of a story.

The reader should be able to flow from chapter to chapter without getting confused.

But trying to *write* this way - I couldn't make it work. Nothing fit together well in my chapters. I couldn't figure out how to go from place to place without writing a bunch of needless exposition, and the transitions were all over the place.

Man, it was a mess. A clunky, bloated mess. The chapters jumped around and weren't cohesive, the timeline got wonky bouncing around so much, and even as the writer, I'd lose my place. Chapters ended and started abruptly.

Trying to figure out how to make my chapters work had me stuck for a while.

But then, I started studying how screenplays were written. Beat by beat, Scene by scene. Act by act. Lots of dialog.

I started to understand the parallel in books. Good writing and good editing should make the mechanics of the story almost invisible to the audience or reader. I started watching movies differently - looking for the energetic markers of the story.

There are conventions to screenwriting that apply beautifully to memoir. Understanding what a beat is, knowing how long a scene should be, and where it should be in relation to the overall story.

As I learned about story structure, and had my mind blown, I found a diagram called the Archplot Structure, compiled by writer Ingrid Sundberg. After studying it, I was completely intrigued. (visit my website resources page for the link to the diagram.)

So, just for fun, I printed a few copies of the diagram and plotted out the parts of the story along the timeline by hand. Suddenly I could see my pattern – the story arc, the challenges, the high's and low's, the final conflict and resolution. I actually had to choose between a few different places to begin my story, which in turn gave me choices about the middle and the end.

It's funny, though, once I mapped it out and had my parts in order in the next draft - I didn't need the diagram anymore. I looked at it a few times in the beginning, but then it got buried in a stack of documents and I found it again a year after I published the book.

And the book ended up really close to the diagram work that I'd done years before. Using the diagram helped me work out a few problems and find the energetic markers of the story.

Chapter Seventeen

The Slice and Dice

During the time I discovered story shapes, and started thinking about scenes instead of chapters, I also stumbled across the work of Shawn Coyne and the *Story Grid* method.

I trusted what showed up, so I started reading transcripts of his podcast with Tim Grahl. Then, I bought his book just to have on hand. It felt like the right thing to do since I got SO MUCH great information from the free podcast.

Anyways, Shawn Coyne approaches the topic of book editing with a very logical, data driven, non-intuitive method of using a spreadsheet.

Pardon me, say what?

OK, I know. I can feel you cringe.

The thought of a spreadsheet might strike fear into the hearts of some writers, but I loved the idea. What the heck - I mean, who's afraid of a little data, right? I had 120,000 words drafted already, a beast that needed edited. I didn't even know how to approach editing, and I'm a curious person. I like playing with ideas.

And this idea intrigued me.

I was ready to try a little reverse engineering. I wanted to see how it all shook out, and how I might improve what I had.

BTW - It was at this stage that I started to push a little on the story. I needed to extract some information from it so I could make it better. This is when your book really starts talking to you, and a conversation ensues.

I'm not a spreadsheet person, but I managed to put together a *really* basic spreadsheet. It wasn't EXACTLY what Shawn Coyne prescribed, but it was good enough. I printed out my big bulky manuscript and tore it up and stapled it into what I thought were scenes and jotted notes about each scene onto stickies.

With the stack of stickied papers in front of me, I plugged everything into the spreadsheet, including word count, setting, year, focus, point of scene, people in the scene, and polarity – whether the scene ended at a high point or a low point. I had about 140 scenes. It took me two full days to do it.

And holy cow - WOW. Seeing that spreadsheet, my brain lit up like a Christmas tree. Suddenly, I saw what wasn't working with my story. One scene about something unimportant was 2500 words, and another scene about a huge event in my life was only 250 words. Yikes.

I saw my gaps, I saw where I had written a similar paragraph explaining the same thing in three different places, I saw where I needed to write more, and I saw which scenes I could move around or cut.

I found my transitions, my flow, my theme. It was a birds' eye view of the story, but the details it revealed about the structural problems were very, very granular. It was like x-ray vision aimed at the bones of the story.

All from a spreadsheet. Who knew?

Your mileage may vary, obviously.

Not everyone will be excited about plotting on a spreadsheet, and I totally get it.

If it intrigues you, do it. If not, skip it.

This worked for me and gave me actionable information about my story – and other than buying an optional book for my bookshelf, I didn't have to pay an expert to do it. I could see it with my own eyes.

Shawn Coyne's methods showed up at the exact moment I was struggling with the issue, so it seemed obvious that I should pay attention to it. Books, concepts, and people that show up at the right time are there to teach you.

Being open to different ways of thinking about your story and being willing to work with what shows up will also unlock your writing.

Curiosity, playfulness, and a bit of detachment from your own fear or ego about the outcome of this method can go a long way towards improving a book.

Just because it was hard to write up to this point doesn't mean that it's good, or that it's done.

Good editing can cure so many problems in your story, so commit to it.

Being analytical about the bones of the story allows the intuition to fill in the muscles and flesh. Dream by dream, sign by sign, scene by scene. You'll know where to put that information.

More Magic Keys.

So, think of scenes, FIRST.

Collect those scenes into chapters, LATER.

When you see your story as scenes and do a little spreadsheet work, when you identify your transition points and natural pauses in the story, when you find connections between scenes that you hadn't seen before - you'll find that the chapters will come together naturally and organically. The chapters will almost organize themselves.

Chapter Eighteen

Action Hack

They say the first draft of a book is you telling yourself the story, and this was very true for me. Gosh, I blathered on. But once I started thinking in terms of scenes, I also started thinking in terms of action.

I didn't know exactly what was meant by "action". I just knew I needed more of it. How does one move the reader through the story? I had no idea, really.

But I started to be aware of the passive language and endless explanation and backstory in my first draft. There wasn't nearly enough dialog, and what was there was clunky.

I wanted to bring the reader right there with me, into the scene, almost like they were watching a movie.

So, instead of taking classes or reading endless advice about "how to" - I took a shortcut.

I reprogrammed my brain a bit. I taught myself how to write differently than what I had been doing up to this point.

It was actually pretty easy to make this shift.

It might be one of my favorite hacks, ever.

I found an action-packed memoir I loved by a writer who inspired me, and I hand-copied the first chapter of her book, word for word, until I felt comfortable writing in that way. I used the rhythm of her language to ground me, to let my brain settle into a pattern.

Then, I took every scene in my own book, and I rewrote it all in an active voice in a similar style to what I had practiced – and voila! It started getting easier and easier to write in an active voice and in a forward motion through the story.

If I started again with the passive language and the yada-yada, I'd refer to my handwriting, read it out loud, maybe copy a bit more, and get back on track.

Using another writer's work as a template is like using training wheels. Just get the feel for it, and then you're suddenly off down the street with wind in your hair, without the training wheels - and you don't even know it.

Using another writer's work helped keep my tenses correct, it was a template for learning how to write dialog and pace the scenes, and I studied how she transitioned between chapters.

You don't need a college degree or any special talents to do this.

Nope, not at all.

Just copy your favorite good writing by hand and then apply that pattern to your own.

If we think in terms of energy and resonance, you are trying to "match frequency". You will level up your writing by matching the energy of the type of book you want to write, and the type of writer you want to be.

Reading it is great, but if you want it to *really* sink in, try copying a few paragraphs of your favorite book by hand if you are able. Let it flow from the fingers grasping the pen, up your arm and into your heart and arteries and spinal cord and straight into your brain.

Let that book energy infuse you.

Seriously, this primes the brain, creates a bit of muscle memory, and allows your work to start matching the vision you have for it.

And don't worry, your own voice and story will shine right through once you apply this to your own work. Once you get the mechanics down and find your groove, your voice will be undeniable.

It was Cheryl Strayed's *Wild*, by the way, the book that inspired me. A memoir about a woman alone on an adventure – it was very similar to my story, although a totally different setting.

Her active voice, her pacing and transitions, and her visually descriptive self-awareness, her humor, and her strength and vulnerability – all of it resonated deeply with me. We were close in age and with the same astrological sign. Although I've had many other writing "muses" over the years, it was with her that I felt most connected with when it came to writing my own book.

So if you find inspiration and deep resonance in another author's work, pay attention.

It may hold another Magic Key for you.

Chapter Nineteen

Ready, or Not

As I mentioned earlier, I've worked with writers as a writing coach/morale supporter to help get their books done and out into the world. I was contacted by someone last year who wanted to write a memoir.

She'd started off wanting to write about her career in show business and her mental health struggles, but as she started talking to family and friends over the following months, some very painful, awful things were revealed to her.

When she contacted me again, things had changed. Her tone was different, defiant, with a "screw them all" thrown in for good measure. She spoke of, "showing them", and "getting revenge for all the betrayals". Nobody messed with her this way! She was ready to name names.

She told me that her memoir was going to be a New York Times best seller because she was a fantastic writer who deserved a movie deal based on the brilliant premise she had come up with for this not-yet-attempted memoir. She was already planning a book tour and talk show appearances. Ellen was going to love her stories!

Oh boy. I was pretty shocked at how she had pivoted. She was triggered and was obviously in the middle of a crisis. This was way, WAY out of my league as a writing coach. I felt bad for the place she was in, and while I am not a mental health professional, I do feel it's important to be as honest and straightforward as I can be with my clients.

I explained that it was important to take a bit of time to heal and process what had been revealed to her. Maybe a few weeks with her family, time with her therapist (I knew she went regularly). Time to be still and not push. I explained that her strong emotions suggested that it would be a good time to journal, digest, and understand this new information. Starting a memoir right now might be too soon.

She had to let those strong emotions settle down for a while so that she could approach her memoir from a more neutral and detached place.

Of course, she didn't want to hear this. How dare I judge her emotional state? She cussed me out, called me a word, and hung up on me. Thank goodness, though. She did us both a favor.

The energy she wanted to put out into the world was not positive, helpful or inspiring. I understand that we all process pain differently, but this revenge energy was dark, angry, and self-centered. Mean, ugly, hurtful, vindictive, and narcissistic.

It's not a vibe that I can vibe with, AT ALL.

Dealing with her on that phone call almost made me physically ill. Energy is contagious, right?

Despite how it ended, that client taught me something super valuable, and I'm writing about that, here:

YOU HAVE TO BE READY TO WRITE YOUR MEMOIR, AND IT CAN'T BE FOR VENGEANCE.

If your reaction to new information is to lash out and be unkind to people - you are not in a good energetic place to start the laboring on a memoir. You need some time. You need to come back to the center. Ego and revenge have no place here.

I mean, you're going to carry that anger and other crap around for two or three or five years while you write a book?

It's SO toxic - both to yourself and to the world at large. There is an energetic cost to getting revenge. It costs you in the end. You end up paying a price, and it can be steep. Your dignity, your honor, your health, and your reputation are at stake. Revenge doesn't age well or serve your long-term interests.

This can be deeply healing work, a vision quest of sorts, and there may be moments that trigger your emotions, which is totally expected. The writing can and will stir up those deep, muddy waters, and you'll need a moment, or a day, or a week, to digest and work through those feelings.

You are human. Please pause and take the time you need. Detach a bit.

The key is to examine those feelings, use them to inform the writing, and move on with the story. Allow yourself the space to process and digest - but don't get bogged down in the weeds.

Memoir forces you to excavate, to connect the ordinary to the extraordinary. But when you hold too tight to your own pain and to old emotional patterns and triggers, you don't have the room you need to expand into the bigger story that will impact others in a positive way.

Every bit of information you receive, every connection you make, every revelation you have during this process is serving your book in some way. Honor those things, appreciate them, however painful they are. Then write them down and keep moving forward.

Magic and good energy is attracted to light, to expansion, to healing, gratitude, forgiveness, and love - and it is actively repelled by ego, revenge, closed hearts and perpetual victimhood.

And if you are operating with the idea that we are all transmitters and receivers, you'll know that this dark energy is not the kind of energy you want to put out into the world.

You are called to share the story because you want it to serve others in some way - to inform, entertain, enlighten, inspire. So, if you are still torn up and triggered over stuff that happened to you - even years ago - then getting on another emotional roller coaster by starting a memoir right now is probably too soon.

Even funny, lighthearted stories can have a dark underbelly. Family drama, betrayal, addiction, violence, heartbreak? A memoir will dredge up the ugly stuff, so be sure you're ready, emotionally, to process it.

There is a big undercurrent of forgiveness when writing a memoir. There is just a lot of stuff you won't be able to make sense of or explain, and the only way to carry on is to accept it for what it was: a shitty situation. Write about it as best you can, with empathy for yourself.

Because that's what's happening here - you're forgiving yourself.

Of course you will feel moments of grief and anger - or you may cycle through a whole range of emotions as you write - all of this is totally normal. You are literally releasing these emotions from your body into the book. Transmutation.

You are liberating them from your body and psyche towards a higher purpose, in service to humanity.

And when you're on fire with the writing and you finish a good writing session and you wrangle those tough emotions into a powerful scene - there can be a sense of giddiness, of being high, or having had a good, almost-orgasmic release.

It almost feels like love. Like falling in love, being in love, making love.

Guess what? Writing is an act of love. *Writing is an act of love*

Because as you process through anger and grief, what comes next and eventually is love, peace, and enlightenment.

You are a CREATOR now, in charge of the world you're creating in your book. You are making conscious and unconscious choices about the energetic signature of the book.

So, mind your energy. Make it a force of love, peace, and enlightenment. When you're ready to start writing your memoir, you will:

Forgive Others.

Find the Good.

See the Humor.

Write with Love. (Even about the bad, ugly, awful stuff)

Be Fierce.

Be Brave.

Be Truthful.

Explain how you changed.

But have mercy.

Especially for yourself

As for others and how they treated you - be as kind as you can be.

Chapter Twenty

People are People

What helped me with writing about certain people - family, friends, old bosses, bad boyfriends - was to view them as characters. I had to detach a bit from the emotion I felt about them, whether good or bad. I really tried to describe their actions, behaviors and appearances in ways that would convey the essence of them to my reader in a truthful way.

And you'll have to make some decisions about these things, especially about how you want to handle the shitty stuff - especially shitty people.

But even if a person treated you poorly in real life, I would encourage you to view them as teachers. You learned something from them. They taught you a valuable lesson. You grew as a person from your experience with them. Your worldview changed.

Try and find gratitude in your heart for those lessons. If you can't love the actual person who treated you poorly, do try and love the character you're creating from their template. Personality traits, dialog, appearance - use these things to advance your story and describe what you were dealing with.

In other words, make them serve your story. Put them to work for you.

Even if they were a monster to you in real life, in your book, they are under your control. You create the narrative here, and how you want to present it.

As imperfect and bad as it was, you can learn to love your villains. But you'll have to dig and digest it all and understand that they are now characters in your story.

You'll be doing this with yourself, as well. You'll look back and try to make sense of it. What kind of kid you were, how your parents affected you, how you processed trauma. You will definitely want to hold love and mercy in your heart for that younger, more innocent version of yourself.

Because in many ways, you are writing for your younger self - to explain it all and make sense of what happened. When you detach from the emotion and really tell the story of your transformation - you'll see those crappy people and bad situations are huge gifts to you now.

Chapter Twenty-One

Big Decisions and Intuitive Guessing

There are a lot of decisions to make when you're writing a memoir.

If you're still in contact with people who will appear in your story, and assuming you're still on good terms, it's always a nice gesture to inform them of your intentions to write about them. This is also a good way to check if they have any feedback, random memories, or a preference of how they'll appear in the book.

For instance, one of my friends works in classified government situations. After talking with them, I made sure it was ok to use their real name in the book.

You don't have to ask permission for every dang thing, but you don't want to be a jerk either. If you're operating from a place of love and integrity, you won't have a problem navigating this.

If someone treated you poorly and you think they should be named, be careful about how you approach this. I am not a lawyer, and this is not legal advice. Just make sure what you are writing is truthful, and that you aren't putting yourself in any legal jeopardy.

Sometimes, of course, they SHOULD be named. Many other times - it won't matter. You are writing your truth. The energy of their actions and behaviors will carry over in your story, no matter what name you give them.

For the sake of clarity and making my book readable, I did decide to root out duplicate names. It turns out I had three Matt's, two Tracy's, two Kathy's and two Aaron's in my life, and all of them were important to the story in some way.

But I also knew that using their real names throughout the book would be confusing to the reader. So, I made this general decision: The most important Matt, Tracy, Kathy, and Aaron would stay themselves and keep their names. The others got a slight name change.

For example, the Aaron who was my first boyfriend and true love - stayed Aaron. The Aaron who was my roommate for a few months in a big city and had since passed away many years ago? I used his middle name and called it good enough.

You may also decide not to name certain people at all, or to keep them anonymous through a name change. If you're not in contact, and you're not sure, and you don't want to cause upheaval in their life by revealing past indiscretions or trauma, then err on the side of a name change and/or anonymity.

For instance, I have a past boyfriend who is happily married with children, is semi-famous, and we aren't in contact (although we still have mutual friends and we left things on good terms.) I changed his name to keep him anonymous, and to respect his wife and children. This seemed much more reasonable than trying to track him down, explain myself, and seek permission and validation - all for two paragraphs in the book about stuff that happened 30 years ago.

From my own experience, it took many, many drafts to figure out how I wanted to handle each situation, especially when it came to people.

Because, as the story evolved, so did my perspective. My feelings about certain things evolved.

For instance, one character in early drafts was a surly, know-it-all asshole. By the time the book was published, he was a no BS kind of guy who pushed me to learn new skills and taught me a huge, meaningful lesson that still affects me today.

But I didn't figure this out until later drafts, when I could put him, and what I had learned from him, into a bigger, deeper context in the story arc.

78

In other words, I kind of had to find the love for him. I had to look for it. Once I realized what he had taught me, though, I was grateful for it, and it made the awkward situation - and my own shortcomings - much easier to write about.

Other decisions will involve your spotty memory and how to "write around" it. While memoir is supposed to be a true story or account of a time in your life, there are going to be moments where you will not remember a key detail - or you feel completely blank on a question that needs answered.

Sometimes you'll be 98% certain on something, but that 2% keeps bugging you.

That's OK. Memoir does give you a little wiggle room with the truth - as I discussed earlier with my multiple-name dilemma. And where you don't know for sure you can intuitively guess, as long as you're not being deceitful. As long as you're keeping to the spirit of the story, it won't matter whether it was Coors or Bud Light, Nike or Adidas.

Sometimes, if you wait long enough, you'll find the answer to your questions. Or things will come to you in a dream, or something will trigger a memory or the right person will appear so you can ask.

And while you don't always get validation or confirmation about your intuitive guesses, when you do, expect to be surprised at how spot on they were.

Chapter Twenty-Two

Dealing with Pauses

I live in Arizona, and I love to explore this beautiful, magical state. When I picture myself writing a book, I visualize being on a long, hot hike out in the Superstition Mountains. The trail is rocky and steep at times, but I'm surrounded by beautiful russet rocks, ancient petroglyphs, majestic cactus and blue sky. Running water from deep springs and shade trees appear on occasion. When you come across it, it's impossible not to be grateful for the small oasis. Anyone who hikes in the desert knows that it's important to stop, hydrate, and rest when you can.

There is a lot of traditional productivity advice that urges writers to write every day, no matter what, and that you're not a "real" writer if you aren't writing like a machine. There is also some mythology around what people call "writer's block". Some say it doesn't exist, some are plagued with it for years, others think it's just laziness.

What I've come to find out about writers is that most writers get stuck and/or must pause the writing at some point along the way. Even professional, productive, and successful writers get stuck sometimes, or are forced to take a break from a project on occasion.

Guess what? Totally normal.

Maybe it's something as simple as a family vacation or an illness that interrupts the flow. Maybe it's because you've just completed a harrowing first draft and need a breather. Maybe you need to take a summer off for the kids, or you just had a baby. Maybe it's just good old anxiety, bolstered by a fear of the unknown. Maybe you just talked to an old friend who clued you in on details that you had no idea of, and you're trying to reconcile it in your mind.

All of these things might pause your writing for a spell, and all of these things are OK, and probably even necessary, especially when writing a memoir or personal narrative.

One needs to sit with the things that come up. One needs to gut-check themselves before writing something painful and truthful. We are human, not robot writing machines. We need to take care of ourselves.

Pauses in your writing can be incredibly productive. The trick is to accept the pauses as just a part of the process of writing a book. You are digesting, incubating, ruminating. Again, it's the concept of productive procrastination.

You are paused, not blocked. You're doing internal work. Allow yourself the time you need.

And as a side note: for goodness' sake, stop talking to everyone about being blocked. Stop saying "I'm blocked", or "I have writer's block". It's bad programming, and your brain will begin to believe it.

You can literally speak things into existence, so don't focus on the negative - *because what you speak will be the result.* Words have power. Speak carefully. Your brain is listening.

The more you verbalize and affirm your perceived block, the more it will become your actual, ingrained reality. I know writers who haven't written in years because they are convinced that they are blocked. That some invisible force is holding them back from writing.

Well, the invisible force is FEAR. We should just call it what it is.

But we have to keep things in perspective. This is a book. You aren't jumping out of an airplane or operating on someone's brain. No one's life is at stake.

Instead of being controlled by an invisible force, just tell yourself you're taking an intentional break. Step away for a bit, breathe, regroup. Nothing to fear.

When you're paused, you are allowing yourself some time to rest. That's it. Don't make it a bigger deal than it is. If there is a block, this will give you time to figure out how to find a way around it.

When I am out of juice and need to step away from the writing, I try to think of it as just a part of the trail I'm hiking on this book journey: *This is a nice place to stop for a bit. I need to catch my breath and rest. I'm going to tend to my blisters and cool off before getting back on the trail. I'm happy to sit under the Cottonwood tree, eat a sandwich, and enjoy the sounds of nature. I'll be ready here again, soon.*

Whatever the reason for your pause, these ebbs are the perfect time to focus on self-care, making sure you get enough sleep, and laughter, and sunshine, and good food, and love. Have a picnic, enjoy your life, take care of what needs tended to, and then you'll be good to go.

The book will still be there, waiting for you. It will call to you. And you'll be thinking about it. Your mind will continue to "chew" on the story - even when you're not actively writing, your subconscious mind will be processing bits and pieces of the book. You'll still be receiving information, digesting it, and making connections. Since you're keeping an imperfect notebook, you can still jot things down, make notes, keep track of your ideas.

And when you're ready, you'll get back on the writing trail and you'll make progress. You should feel no guilt or shame about the slow-down. Writing a book can be a long, hot, challenging hike, and you'll need a pause to rest. Probably even a few times.

It's just normal. It's normal for us intuitive, sensitive types. It's normal for most writers, actually.

Don't worry, friend. You're going to make it. Just don't quit.

Trust yourself to take the breaks you need, and then get back on the writing trail.

There is nothing to fear at all.

Chapter Twenty-Three

Romancing the Intuition

I've been aware of my intuition for a long time, and ever since I was a child I've been fascinated by metaphysics, energy and magic. Growing up, I was intrigued by stories of past lives, alternative history, psychics, ghosts, Big Foot, and other unexplained phenomena. I've just always had a really open mind about this stuff, and my Sicilian heritage reinforced much of it.

As I grew older, I became aware that I had mildly psychic gifts. I have had many, many dreams over the years that have played out in real life in a way that could only be called "precognition". I've been aware many times of a situation or an outcome that I had already dreamed, or sensed. I just "know" things about people and situations. It's like I download information from somewhere and store it in my hard drive.

It's not something I can really control or direct at this point, but I am aware that I can prime the pump in some ways to help my intuition flow more freely.

I want these bits of information to flow without the impediment of logic or organization, so that they come through in a pure form. I want to tap into that subconscious wisdom.

I can apply logic to these bits AFTER I've received, if necessary.

When it comes to writing, in some way, you are acting upon a vision, or an idea you have in your head, or a feeling you're trying to convey. You may not be aware of any of this yet - but as you keep going deeper into the story, you'll find yourself asking more questions than your logical, rational, conscious brain can figure out.

So, as you become aware that there are things you are going to have to figure out just beyond the edge of logic - you'll start getting clues. Don't judge them or place value on anything - just observe, be aware, notice patterns. This is why it's helpful to have a notebook to jot things down as they come.

Things like:

Random songs that remind you of someone or something, a time or a place. Or, you'll hear the same song three different times during the day and later someone mentions the artist. Is there something there? Does the song, or the lyrics, or the artist have a message or a memory for you that relates to your story?

Animals, critters, birds that show up randomly, or in patterns. For instance, one very busy, chaotic week I was stalked by a beautiful praying mantis who kept appearing on my patio screen door, even after relocating her to a wildflower patch multiple times. Then I investigated the symbolism of the praying mantis - stillness, calm, introspection - and it was a perfect reminder for me to step back and slow down a bit. She kept showing up until I got the message. What do your animal friends represent to you when they show up?

Numbers. There are times when I wake up at the same time every day - 4:44am - or when I keep seeing the number 11 - and for a while it kind of boggled me. But now I think it is the very subtlest reminder from the Universe to pay attention. A small nudge making you notice the pattern. Do certain numbers keep showing up? Does it mean anything to you? What other synchronicities do you notice?

Who are you attracting? As I progressed through my book and coaching practice, I realized that I was attracting a certain type of person into my sphere. Not that it was bad or good - but it was a pattern I recognized after about five of the same energetic-types found me. It made me more mindful of what I was putting out there, and how to use it as a strength to connect with more people. I was also able to attract to me the people I most needed, when I needed them - even if it was just their books, or a podcast, or an article that showed up right on time.

Using Social Media. What I find most intriguing about social media is that over the years, a few accounts that I follow seem to randomly post about the EXACT thing I am feeling or writing about that day. It gets to be a little spooky, honestly, but it is SO very cool to be able to experience the energy this way. While it may seem that we are only superficially connected to others on social media, in truth, it's a reminder that we are all *deeply* connected to each other by a larger hive-mind or collective. Does your feed ever have any clues or answers or inspiration for you?

Your body is telling you. Muscle aches, sore throat, foot problems? Are any of these related to your story? Do you ever pay attention to how your body feels when you're thinking or writing about a certain event? Any childhood injuries or trauma that acts up? There's an old saying: The body keeps the score. When you're releasing old energy through writing your book, your body may also be releasing old energy and revealing clues to you. Pay attention to what hurts and ask it what it's related to and how you can help resolve the pain. This dialog may hold deep revelations - and healing - for you.

Some of the things that worked to keep my brain in a flowing, receptive state:

A notebook to jot things down, as discussed earlier.

Routine or ritual. I know I can't write every day, but I know I have Friday mornings to myself, so I try to make the most of it. I like to make sure I have my candles lit, a cup of coffee and a glass of water nearby, that the dog has been fed and walked so she isn't too hyper, and that I have my music playlist going.

I don't care about word count at all, I just want to dive in and do what I can do for as long as I can go that session. I try to start a load of laundry, which takes exactly 45 minutes in the washer, which is about when I need to stretch my legs. It also makes me feel less guilty about taking the time to write the book - when I could be doing laundry AND writing the book. 3 or 4 loads of laundry with 10-minute breaks in between can add up to a very productive writing session.

The music playlist. Music was crucial for me. I was writing a rock n' roll memoir, so the music was a central character in my story in some ways. Putting on a good playlist, or a Pandora station that pulled a random, yet curated, soundtrack for each writing session is part of my routine. Some people prefer to work in silence, or while listening to binaural beats. You do you. Music is also a story, and depending on the type of music you listen to - you'll come to see the shape of music as well. It may also affect the energy of the book you're working on while listening to it - so be intentional, and inspired.

Sacred space. I think every writer needs a special spot - a sacred space for their writing. I wish I could tell you that I had my own perfect serene and private office, but I don't - and until my kids are grown and out of the house, I won't have an extra bedroom to spare for a while.

So, I make do. I have a spot near the patio door, between the kitchen and living room, in a smallish open-concept house. It has one wall with shelving, and no doors. The fridge is 5 feet away from my chair in one direction, the family-room sofa 5 feet away in the other direction.

However - this is MY SPOT. My crystals, trinkets, animals, pictures, plants, and other energetic talismans are all around me. I bought a beautiful rug for my feet and a pretty lamp. My writing and metaphysical books are nearby, as are my Tarot cards, candles, and artwork. I have a comfy chair and a footrest. It is the only spot I have in the house, so I keep it tidy and pretty and ready for me.

Whenever I sit in my chair, I feel nothing but good energy and creative love, supported with things that inspire me. My husband and kids might be watching a scary spider movie a few feet away on the sofa - but I'm in my sacred space, doing the sacred work. Earbuds and a music playlist can really help if your writing spot isn't ideal.

The big advantage to my particular spot is that snacks are mere steps away.

Try and find a space for your own creative work, and then fill it with things that inspire you. A pinecone, a pretty rock, a shell from the seashore, your grandmother's rosary, pictures of your ancestors, postcards, dried flowers, a shark's tooth? All of it is fair game in your spot. Whatever helps you romance your intuition and support your creativity.

Chapter Twenty-Four

Other Magic Keys

I mentioned earlier taking a **Myers-Briggs** personality test. I'm a big fan of "artist, know thyself" so understanding the patterns of personality are valuable to me. The same goes for Enneagram, and any other test that might show your dominant traits, gifts, and tendencies. This helped me understand how different we all are from each other, and how certain personality types process information. I love the patterns of human behavior.

The same goes for understanding the basics of **astrology.** I studied the concepts for many years and became familiar with my own chart. I understand the patterns and archetypes represented by the astrological signs and symbols and how they are compatible or discordant. When you dive a little deeper,

Patterns of human behavior

sometimes you can see patterns in your own characters and story.

For instance, I am a Virgo. I revealed that almost every person I was close to in my book were also Virgos. It was so strange, almost bizarre, really. I've also noticed that every Aquarius person that I've ever known is left-handed. I don't know what it means, other than it's a pattern I notice and find curious.

I also appreciate knowing the phases of the moon and planets and how they affect me. Mercury retrogrades affect things almost always, and full moons wreck my sleep - but I often have the best dreams during these transitions.

I am a big, big fan of my dream world, so I do employ some techniques for **lucid dreaming,** such as asking myself the specific question that needs answered, or preparing to have a conversation with someone I'm hoping to see in my dream, like I did with my friend, Kevin.

I also dream of places, rooms, landscapes that I visit again and again. I wander around houses and cities and shorelines hoping to learn more about this "place" and why I'm there in my dream.

Sometimes, when I dream about real places, I find them on Google Maps and get down to street level to really look around to try and immerse myself to see if it triggers anything in my dreams.

Nutritional deficiencies can wreck your sleep and brain health, and if you're middle-aged like me, I can't urge you enough to get your blood work checked and on a few supplements that will enhance your synapsis and moods.

Obviously, talk to your doctor or naturopath. For me, it was magnesium, B vitamins, and vitamin D. These deficiencies are so common in our modern society, and they can mimic many other conditions, including anxiety, depression, and memory problems. When I take these supplements at night, I have incredible dreams and deeper, less disturbed sleep. And I feel better during the day, with lessened anxiety.

Hydrate with good, mineral rich water. So much brain fog can be cured with proper hydration. And also make sure you **move your body.** If you don't have a regular routine, just take a walk, walk the dog, go for a bike-ride, or a hike, or do some yoga or intentional stretching. Keeping your body limber and hydrated also keeps the brain limber and unclogged. Having a glass of water before my coffee in the morning along with 10 minutes of stretching in my kitchen seems to set my whole day up for good writing flow. And it turns out my friend Sam was right about the **carbs.** I think so much clearer when I keep them in check. But that might be a middle-age thing, and not necessarily a writer thing.

And of course, I have to mention my **Tarot** deck. I don't know if it can tell your fortune or predict your future, but Tarot can reveal keys, symbols, and patterns that spark your deepest insights and can help you unlock your creativity.

I purchased my first deck 30 years ago and have studied it ever since. Something about the mystery of it fascinates me. The cards seem to talk to me, and they open doorways in my minds' eye.

I understand that there are some misconceptions about Tarot, and you may or may not be comfortable using it or seeking out a Tarot advisor, but if it resonates with you, dig around a little bit and explore.

Each card has an energetic story to tell that may hold some clues for you on your writing journey. The best way to find a deck to use is to actually look at the images and artwork to see if they speak to you in some way. A deck you connect with visually and energetically is a deck that will work for you.

I pull cards a few times a week just to check in, to see what parallels are revealed, to see if there is anything that feels like an energetic hit. A few cards reminded me of actual people or situations, and act as guideposts, almost.

I recently started reading cards for a few select clients who have asked me to advise them in regard to their writing and creative lives, and it's a really great way to unlock patterns that might be holding you back.

The cards can open doorways in your mind that can help you answer the thing that you're wondering about, or to affirm a direction you're going, or to illuminate something deep in your psyche, or to help you recognize a habit of mind that is no longer serving you.

I've come to trust my Tarot deck as my own personal writing advisor, another type of coach.

I can ask my deck questions that no one else can answer and the insights I gain are invaluable.

Is it magic? I don't know. I don't care. I just know it works.

Chapter Twenty-Five

The Last Mile

Writing a book can be a long and lonely hike, but it doesn't have to be. You can find help, encouragement, and inspiration along the way.

I can't tell you how long your memoir journey will last or where it will take you, but if you're committed to the path it will be one of the most profound and rewarding things you'll ever do.

You owe it to the story to not leave it unwritten. You can't just leave it out there in the cold. It's part of you, and to neglect the call to write it is to neglect your own heart.

So find a way to write your book.

I'm almost 50 years old, and I've done a lot of things in my life. Finally writing and publishing my first book was a HUGELY awesome thing. I am not the same person I was. This is a transformational experience. I was not only birthing a book but a whole new version of myself.

Writing the book brought a community of people together and reconnected me with lifelong friends. I was able to document my experiences for future generations. What a gift it's been to do this work.

And one of the most satisfying things is hearing from people about how much they enjoyed the story, and how they were able to escape back to a time and a place that they remember as fondly as I did.

Look, we all have stories to tell. If you're not sure how you're supposed to do it, look around. Ask questions. Seek out help. Use what resonates with you. There is no one right way. You just need to find your way.

Trust that this is possible because it *totally* is.

If you're called to write your story, trust that you have the tools to do it. **The Universe wouldn't put it on your heart if you didn't have the ability to write the book.**

Trust your intuition and dreams. Trust your ancestors, trust your story, trust the process, and trust yourself. Write down what it is you need, what you hope for, how you can serve. And then trust what shows up.

Go out into the wild forest with your ax and wheelbarrow and gather your materials. Write that first draft, and then learn to edit and keep working on it until you're done.

None of this advice is new, and I'm no writing expert. But sometimes you need to hear the same things from a slightly different voice – maybe a new writer who has just been through it - in order for things to resonate.

When I finally found that resonance and smashed through my own writing problems, it really did feel like I had been unlocked, released, or liberated in some way.

Discovering what worked for me for my first book felt like a series of Magic Keys that were presented along the path. I gathered them up, unlocked my doors, and documented the process along the way. As a librarian and a writer, sharing resources and helping other writers is just second nature, and is the right thing to do.

And so, I present these Magic Keys to you in hopes that you'll find a way to unlock your own writing, get your book done, and share your story with the world. You CAN do this, and I'm rooting for you.

Thank you for reading, and best wishes to you, writing friends. If this book resonated with you, please consider supporting independent authors and leave a review on Amazon.

If you'd like to know more about memoir, writing, intuition, or my coaching services, visit me at annamarieobrien.com where you can sign up for my newsletter.

Connect with me:
- Instagram @metalheadlibrarian or
- Twitter @annamarieobrien

And if this book helped you in some profound way, I'd love to hear about it. Email me at annamarieobrien@gmail.com.

This book is dedicated
to my husband, Jim. Thank you for
everything, my love.